VODOUN

Why African-Americans Fear Their Cosmogenetic Paths to God
An Illustrated History of Racism and Religious Persecution in America

Mama Zogbé
Chief Hounon-Amengansie

This booklet is part of a series towards the Reclamation of the Religious Heritage of the Diaspora Project

Mami Wata Healers Society of North America Inc.,
Martinez, GA 30907

Library of Congress Cataloging in Publication Data

Hunter-Hindrew, Vivian
Why African-Americans Fear Their Cosmogenetic Paths to God:
An Illustrated History of Racism and Religious Persecution in America
Vivian Hunter-Hindrew
Bibliography.
Appendix.
Includes Index & Glossary.
ISBN 0-9716245-9-3.

Copyright © First Printing 2007 by Vivian Hunter-Hindrew.

All rights reserved. No part of this work may be reproduced or transmitted in any form by any means, electronic or mechanical, including photocopying and recording, or by any information storage or retrieval systems, except as may be expressly permitted by the current Copyright Act, or in writing by the author.

Mami Wata when in use with logo (front cover) is a federally registered trademark of the *Mami Wata Healers Society of North America Inc.*, It is registered under #T-20963, with the United States Department of Commence and Trademark Office. When in use with the logo (front cover) Mami Wata® is federally protected both as a product name and organizational logo, No claim is made to the exclusive right to use MAMI WATA apart from the mark as shown on the front cover or with any symbol connected as a trademark of the Mami Wata Healers Society. It is therefore a violation to use the aforementioned name in conjunction with the logo to market products, or to render services of any kind without the express permission of the trademark owner.

Requests for such permission should be addressed to:

Mami Wata Healers Society of North America Inc.,
P.O. Box 211281
Martinez, GA 30907
Hqts: (706) 267-3324
Fax: (706) 863-4886
Website: www.mamiwata.com
Email: *MWHS@mamiwata.com*

Manufactured in the United States of America..
Back Cover Design: *Mami Wata Society Logo*, by Mama Zogbé (Vivian Hunter-Hindrew).

FORWARD

It has been nearly half a century since the Civil Rights Movement. It is understood by most scholars that the struggle for human dignity came at a heavy price, in which the descendants of the enslaved are still paying today. In spite of the "advances" in social and human rights, the Black family is still struggling to survive as a fundamental cultural unit. More than half of Black children are growing-up without fathers. Black men are incarcerated into the for-profit prison-industrial-complex in disproportionate numbers. The number of Black American businesses has actually decreased, and their profits have little to no economic and political impact on the greater community. Black children are still being "educated" in poorly funded and staffed schools, that teach a largely Eurocentric curriculum in which they learn little to nothing about themselves. The impact of obesity, violence, homelessness, mental illness, drugs, Aids, and other social and biological diseases are impacting the Black community without any relief in sight.
   The dwindling Black middle-class remains isolated and alienated in white suburbs in their attempts to offer a "better life" for their *own* children. Literally millions of Black children are being mis-diagnosed as *attention-deficient*, and are heavily medicated. Black men and women suffer from mental and spiritual illnesses without realizing its African spiritual roots. Yet, the one major factor that they all boast in common is that they are *Christian* or *Muslim*. The two major dogmatic western religious traditions which claimed to "save" them from their African barbarity; *elevating* them into the global human spiritual family.

Few in the Diaspora question the myth that the Africans enslaved to build the economic foundation of America were Christians. Some actually believe that being forced to serve a western Christian god was the best thing that happened out of the horrors of slavery(!). Few are even aware that before there was the *"war on drugs,"* there was a vicious, unrelenting serious *"war on African religious practices,"* in **America.** A spiritual and cultural war in which many lost their lives, and stringent laws were passed forbidding the crafting of drums, ceremonial dances, parades, and other community gatherings in celebration of the ancestors and African spirit. The highly respected body of priestesses and priests were forced underground in order to continue the ancient and powerful tradition of ancestral veneration and services to their clan and totem deities. At the turn of the century, brainwashed free-slaves were converted to Christianity and placed in the pulpit, where they remain today. Their original role was to condition the masses of sharecropping and domestic Blacks to the "new slave theology". Black women, who descend from an ancient past of spiritual autonomy and authority in Africa, were now forced into subservient roles in the Western Christian churches. A social ploy designed to temper their *insurrectionists fires.*

The racists and demeaning imagery of the Vodoun and other African religions practiced by Blacks in America, stood side-by-side with the Black face minstrels, and other disparaging images of Blacks. New generations of Black s were born, *longing to be free,* shamefully rejected the spiritual knowledge of their ancestors as "superstitious" and refused the call of their family deities.

This ancestral disruption has caused devastating consequences for the Black family. Many whose minds are now riddled with fear and ignorance, have no idea that cutting the Diaspora away from their ancient spiritual roots was the most major *"coup de espirit"* which finally broke the backs and improvised the spirits of Blacks in America. Today, even many educated Blacks who profess a profound knowledge of Africa, secretly reject its religions, without realizing that the state of African religions is the cumulative result of centuries of warfare against Western encroachment, colonialism, and corruption within its own ranks. Until the present, those who undertake the expensive journey of seeking out their ancestral religious rites are often rejected by their "Christian" families, and are secretly mocked as "*strange*" "*evil*" and even *insane*.

Why is it taking the Black community so long to recognize their cosmogenetic (bio-spiritual) connection to their ancient ancestors and deities? How is it possible that Africentric scholars can proudly expound upon the lost and hidden glory of Africa, and yet shamefully shudder
at its so-called "*paganism*" "*fetish*" practices, without making the obvious connection between Africa's glory and their gods? How is it possible for the average Black American to deny and fear more than 70,000 years of divine spirit and ancestors that run through their veins? Why has the Diaspora not taken-up the most fundamental human rights struggle of reclaiming the religions that their ancestors brought to America; which formed the most crucial part of themselves as a people? What happened to these African religions in America, and why are African-

Americans searching elsewhere for their salvation, while secretly despising their native African souls? Why has the Diaspora continuing to allowed Hollywood and western Christian evangelicals to define, mis-represent, demonize, and mock the spiritual soul and cultural practices of African religions such as Vodoun ("Voodoo")? It is not possible for these same media forces to mock Islam, Hinduism, Buddhism or any other spiritual traditions in the manner in which they disrespect those of the African. Why does the Diaspora sit passively and allow the public humiliation of their ancestors and gods by themselves (rappers) and other people?

It is said that a picture is worth a thousand words. They can speak and tell a story that America has long ago hidden in its archives of shame. There were many wars fought against the enslaved African to force their compliance. This story, one of the most important, *needs* to told for the countless numbers who are unaware of just how the majority in the Diaspora learned to despise their most sacred spiritual heritage. In the end, it is the Diaspora who has a duty to learn to honor and respect their spiritual history. Re-education and reclamation is the crucial key which can aid in unlocking centuries of fear, ignorance and shame. This brief illustrated history of religious self-hatred it is hoped, can aid in the healing process.

Mama Zogbé,
Chief Hounon-Amengansie,
Mami Wata, Mama Tchamba, Yeveh Vodoun Religion

VODOUN

Why African-Americans Fear Their Cosmogenetic Paths to God
An Illustrated History of Racism and Religious Persecution in America

Fig 1:   John Promis "Paw". 1857-1921.
Prosperous Mami Wata & Vodoun Priest.
Great-great grandfather of Mama Zogbé (author).

"Paw use to take us across this small bridge that he'd built. For years, we'd track on across that bridge, and never thought nothing of it. It was not until later that we realized that it wasn't no bridge at t'all; but a great-big-ole-serpent!"

"You see, in those days, before the White man started clubbing and shooting them to death, they [the serpents] use to grow that big!"

Accused of being a "warlock", Paw was chased into a barn by a group of Christians, who then set it ablaze. Waiting to retrieve his body to parade as an "example" to others, it was never found.   Has been the subject of secret family-lore ever since.

-[Mama Zogbé's] Family-lore

"Here the investigation into the prognathous [ape] race must close . . . leaving the most interesting part, Fetishism, the indigenous religion of the African tribes untouched.
It is the key to the Negro character which is difficult to learn from mere experience."

E.N. Elliot, L.L.D.
"Cotton is King" 1860
Augusta, GA.

TWO HUNDRED YEARS OF RELIGIOUS BIGOTRY

Fig 2: African priestess buffooned and sold as *Americana*. ©The Jim Crow Museum of Racist Memorabilia.

By far, one of the most notoriously under reported iniquities in the annals of slavery and colonialism in Africa and in the New World, was the indiscriminate religious persecution of Africans. In Africa, this carefully planned inquisitorial undertaking, was achieved thru the systematic disparagement, violent torture, social ostracism, imprisonment, and murder of the queen mothers, the priestesses, priests and diviners. Just as in ancient Greece, Asia Minor and Rome, hundreds of African shrines were either destroyed outright, or converted into Christian churches. Along with this wholesale destruction came the deliberate undermining and discrediting of the African sacerdotal authorities, meaning its ancient systems of Eldership and Queenship, which formed the bedrock of African moral, social, religious and cultural life. Many were either manipulated into forcing villagers to accept the corrupted and heavily plagiarized Christian doctrines, while others were viciously attacked and publicly mocked and murdered if they refused.

MYTH OF CHRISTIANIZED AFRICANS

So successful were slaver-holders, Western scholars, and Christian evangelicals of intimately associating African religions with *paganism, witchcraft, satanism, barbarity, primitivism, and cannibalism*, that many sympathetic whites and even black ecclesiastics and abolitionists, omitted its very presence and practices from American history out of respect (they believed) for the African-liberation cause.

American historians have almost completely ignored the widespread presence of African religious practices during their enslavement, and its violent suppression. An omission leading to the false belief that Africans were joyfully *Christianized*, or worst, culturally impoverish and morally bankrupted slates, upon their forced arrival in the New World. The incessant and resounding myth that Africans enslaved in America were already *Christians* or being *Christianized* is one that flies in the face of the growing anecdotal and historical evidence. This history proves that these myths, perpetuated by Christian sympathizers and abolitionists were little more than political, abolitionists fairytales.

In truth, what most abolitionists and Christian sympathizers always knew was as recent as the early 1900's, more than 70-80 percent of African-Americans still adhered to and preferred their native traditional religious practices and folk beliefs. Owing to the nature of the African religious and philosophical make-up, it was nearly impossible for them to separate themselves from their spirituality, without totally shattering their African identity. This fact is acknowledged by Professor Terry Matthews in his thesis <u>The Religion of the Slaves</u>:

Long before their contact with whites, Africans were a strongly religious, and deeply spiritual people."... There certainly may have been an element of truth to these observations about the persistence of African-American spirituality in the face of efforts of whites to erase it. The Ashanti had a folk saying that "No one shows a child the Supreme Being." Although the African's world was populated by a plurality of powers, including the forces of nature and a legion of magical spirits, most tribes believed in a Supreme Being who was viewed as a creator, giver of rain, and sunshine, the all-seeing one, the one who exists by himself. Moreover, traditional African religion made no distinction between the sacred and secular. All of life--not part--was sacred. Nor was there any sense of a division between this life and the one to come. All of life was part of a continuum in which both the living and dead took part.[3]

Matthews eloquently captures the threatening social reality that greatly troubled whites and the plantation aristocracy:

By the standards of the early nineteenth century, African-Americans were said to be "a wretched stock of heathens, in utter darkness of a loathsome pagan idolatry." Various plantation owners expressed the concern that "the superstitions brought from Africa have not been wholly laid aside." Witchcraft, alleged superstitions, and fetishist practices were often cited as evidence that the plantation slave refused to abandon African paganism for American [meaning white] Christianity ... Whites often commented on these "pagan practices," and fetishes, and were threatened by them. As a result, great effort was expended on eradicating these practices ...[4]

WAR AGAINST AFRICAN RELIGIOUS WORSHIP

In America, the very threat of African religious survival, which emphasized the warrior gods, to aid in their fight against forced enslavement, posed a very real fear for whites. Both because of its efficacy, and its disruption of southern cultural values, meaning their [the Africans] perpetual servitude. This fear escalated in to *Code Noir* (*Black Laws*) outlawing almost everything African, especially their religions and languages.

Severely oppressive, these Draconian laws forbade the making of ritual drums, musical instruments, dancing, singing, praying, and even congregating for spiritual worship, except in the presence of a white overseerer. These inhumane laws were justified through a national and state sanctioned Christian cult like culture of racist mockery.

Africans, their persona, culture and religious practices, served as the dichotomous *dark, primitive other* that sanctioned their oppression and enslavement. This atmosphere served to allow the Western world to amass enormous amounts of wealth, and power as they perfected and instituted a political and social meaning for *whiteness* to justify their [and Europes] new found prosperity.

During chattel slavery, especially in the South, African religious traditions were vilified and their active practices outlawed by punishment of heavy penalties, torture, and death. Many priests/ess whom slave owners feared might incite civil disobedience and war (insurrections), were actively sought out and accused of *witchcraft and sorcery*, and publicly tortured and murdered. This sate sanctioned terrorism was meant to set an example of what would befall th e rest should they continue to identify with their African-selves. As a result, African ancestors, and their deities, were forgotten or improperly propitiated. The burial rites of enslaved Africans, their parents and their children, were often shamefully inadequate, or haphazardly performed or outright forbidden.

The unceasing monitoring and active search and destroy missions of the State for any suspicious mound, ritual object, consecrated site, or suspected public gatherings, forced African worship permanently underground. Further, fueled by the degrading and racists images of Hollywood and Christian evangelical condemnation, millions of African-Americans began to reject their most potent system of spiritual knowledge and divine connections with their ancient ancestors and deities.

INHERENT INFERIORITY OF AFRICAN SOUL

In truth, the persecution of Africans and the suppression of their religious practices in America, was not sparked by fear of insurrections as much as it was precipitated by whites who believed, unapologetically, that Africans were lessor evolved humans with *childish minds*. They asserted that the Africans were spawned from *primitive cultures*, nourished by malevolent spirits; and as a result, they could only be saved through perpetual servitude. That is to say:

"... *one-half of the existing commerce and industry depends upon raw products, raised by Africans in servitude. In return for that servitude, the Africans receive civilization and Christianity, in addition to physical support. Without that condition of service, they would be Pagan cannibals.*" [2]

SAVED FROM AFRICAN BARBARISM

Voodoo initiations, ancestor propitiation, holy ceremonies and other sacred rites, acquired its *dark and mysterious* reputation because its adherents had been forced by the State to practice in secret. African religions were categorically rejected around the colonial New World, and its place as the historical source of Christianity and most major systems of divine worship in the world, was concealed and denied and lost forever to its future generations.

Fig 3: Later generations of Black mothers having forgotten their own faiths, were often forced to indoctrinate their children with corrupted Christian doctrines which sanctioned their enslavement and dehumanization. They believed that if they succumbed to the faith of whites, they would be accepted as *brothers in Christ*, and therefore, sparred further humiliation social ostracism and suffering. ©The Jim Crow Museum of Racist Memorabilia.

One of the greatest successes of European religious propaganda was not only to convince the West Africans enslaved in the New World, that they were being *saved* from a *barbarous* system of idolatry, but that their *primitive* systems of worship were a bizarre and shameful aberration from the traditional theology, rituals and customs of those civilizations in North and East Africa and, in turn, the world.

The Christian church acting as the moral arm of the Confederacy, maintained its hegemonic control over other faiths by continuing the successful suppression of all its religious competitors. Since nearly all Christian churches in America supported slavery, they achieved their success by waging a vicious battle of propaganda against all traditional forms of worship. Especially if those empowering traditions interfered with the enslaved African s ability to produce.

FEAR, SHAME & IGNORANCE HAUNTING DIASPORA

By the mid-late 1900s, millions in the diaspora had forgotten how they came to fear, disrespect and to loose the most sacred aspect of their African heritage. The majority, in their desire to lessen the sting of social ostracism and racism, unquestionably embraced the myth of Christianity as being one of the "beneficial rewards" of the forced servitude of their ancestors. Unfortunately, many today have little understanding as to how these conditioned beliefs evolved.

In American, democratic society, which prides itself on religious freedom and self-expression, African religions are the only systems of worship that are still allowed to be universally mocked and buffooned by Hollywood, rap artists, public personalities, and demonized by many Christian evangelists. Many Christians (white and black) even until today, still believe it their divine duty to "convert" Africans and others without regard to their own indigenous faiths. They still view African religions as a product of "*primitive superstition*," and its deities and clergy as agents of "their devil." Millions of dollars are spent by Christian churches on "missionary" work throughout Africa, than on the development of Africa's infra-structure or on her industries ravished by centuries of colonialism, war and corruption.

Fig 4: Many African-Americans whom are now "spooked" by appearances of their ancestral spirits, once understood their mysteries, and did not fear the spirit world. However, whites mistook their respect for not offending the dead as superstitious, ignorance and fear. Often, they would buffoon blacks in newspaper editorials and on popular television. Overtime, in a desperate attempt at assimilation, blacks discarded their complex theologies and ancestral religions in favor of universal white acceptance. ©The Jim Crow Museum of Racist Memorabilia.

IMPLOSION OF WHITES IN AFRICAN RELIGIONS

Within the past two decades, there has been an implosion of whites who have sought refuge under the cloak of African traditional religious practices. Many, ignorant of its history, philosophy, cosmogony and sacred rites, have mistaken them to be the next hierarchal complement to their various pagan, satanic, and gothic practices. This is viewed by the Diaspora, (many who are beginning a new appreciation and study of African spirituality), as a continuation of the cultural vulturization and perpetration of the same racist stereotypes, and are therefore resentful. Many in the Diaspora also express a deep resentment at the presence of whites in African religions, and what they perceive as their arrogance and sense of entitlement to what the Diaspora s believe to be their ancestral birthright. They [whites] on the other hand, often react angrily or are confused and hurt by this rejection.

Part of the problem lies in white s (and others) not having learned or who remain indifferent to, the brutal and violent history of African religious suppression in the West. Because these new generations of whites (and others) are seeking solace, as their more ancient ancestors once sought through African Spirit, they too have an obligation to learn and to understand its history in America, and why the Diaspora might view their presence with caution and suspicion.

JOURNEY INTO AMERICA'S RACIST PAST

To aid in this understanding, the following picto-history offers a brief overview of just how pervasive and widespread the destruction and demonization of African religious culture pervaded American and European culture. Learning this history is critical to an overall understanding of why many in the Diaspora appear so uncomfortable with the present trend of what they perceive as the cultural vulturism, contextual misrepresentation, and the arrogance exhibited by the many whites (and others) whom they feel are merely there to exploit their ancestral traditions.

If these images appear *"emotionally charged,"* one can only imagine what its victims both past and present, were/are experiencing. Perhaps the next battlefront, or the new Civil Rights of the 21st century, might be for religious freedom for all.

Nearly all of the photos are used with the permission of:

John Thorp s (Phd), *The Jim Crow Museum of Racist Memorabilia.*
<http://www.ferris.edu/news/jimcrow>

BLACK WOMEN S *SUFFRAGE*

Fig2: An October 3, 1868 political cartoon from an unknown popular American journal, depicting a mob of protesting white men against a deliberately masculinized Black female suffrage. One man is violently stomping on a pile of books they have previously set-ablaze. On the dress of the White woman is a label which reads "*Southern Democracy*." Written across the hair she has chopped-off the enslaved African woman is the word "*Suffrage*." Hair, has always been viewed as the source of power for women. The statue above them is their rendition of the biblical patriarch, *Moses*, allegedly pointing at the *Ten Commandments*. What is interesting to note, is the symbolism associated with this African woman. She is draped in white cloth, her breast violently exposed, and resting on a lamb or sheep s wool rug. To her left, rests a smoking censor. Her (prophetic) books are being burned, while to her far (bottom) right rests a coiled serpent. All classic ritual symbols of the historical Sibyls. However, to the enemies of her freedom, they are mocking what they believe are symbols of her sorceress spirit symbolizing her *demonic* and *untamed* nature. Qualities which they fear, if unleashed, would *portend moral and spiritual decadence for the whole of puritanical America.*

VILLAGE CHIEF

Fig 3: Village chief. The leopard skin is a sacred symbol in the Vodoun religion, (as it was in India, Afro-Syria, Afro-Babylon, and ancient Egypt). It indicates the totemic lineage of the wearer, possessing the spiritual power and sacred knowledge of the ancestors. Once revered and respected, Europeans of rank, encroaching into the interior of Africa, originally displayed great honor and obeisance to these divine village kings. However, after their successful colonization and control of Africa, and her human and material resources, these demeaning and racist images subsequently followed.

SIMPLE-MINDED AFRICAN

Fig 4a Simple-minded African   Fig 4b: Simple-minded African

Newspaper clipping. Once the Portuguese, French, Germans and British, etc., were assured of their foothold into Africa, it became necessary to create racist propaganda to justify colonialism, exploitation, and slavery. The above scene was typical of Europe and America's collective efforts to undermine the spiritual intellect of Africa's priesthoods. The scene features a local village priest, rushing to inquire of the white priest, Father Joseph about his wife who'd just given birth to an albino child (being carried on her back). The implication being that it is a white baby, that father Joseph might have fathered, but the simple-minded, brutish African, perplexed and not making the connection, rushes to the white priest for an intelligent explanation as to why the baby is white, in which father Joseph explains: *These are the secrets of nature. You have to accept them without understanding them.* This, besides the fact, that historically Africans have been giving birth to albino babies for millennia, and the divinatory powers of the priest inquires of the divinities and Ancestors if such births portend maleficent, or beneficent benefits for the community as well as for the child. It should also be noted that many of these European priests were not actually ordained, but merely merchants posing as such. Because Africans are traditionally tolerant and respectful of all faiths, it was an assured means by which the merchants could gain a foothold and audience directly with the kings. White woman prostitutes would often accompany them posing as the Virgin Mary to seduce the kings. During the ruthless battles between the Europeans over Africa's wealth, whatever it took to acquire a competitive edge in Africa is what many of them resorted to.

"MASAI GIRLS"

Fig 5: Bugs Bunny cartoons were some of the most racist on network television. Here, Bugs Bunny is mocking East African Masai girls.

CANNIBALS

Fig 6: African priests depicted as cannibals. Captions reads: Am having a howling good time.

MORE CANNIBALS

Fig 7:
Caption reads: "*Grand Banquet Tonight*"

Millions of households all across America, and indeed the world, tuned in to MGM, (Metro-Goldwyn-Mayer), and Warner Brother's Studios children cartoons. Almost from the cradle, the impressionable minds of Black children [and the world] were seared with these grotesque images debasing their Blackness, African culture, and religions. Africa and Africans were viewed as uncivilized, and wild jungle, inhabited by Black savages, and cannibals, with a special appetite for Christian whites. This, despite the fact that there are no jungles in Africa, nor has there ever existed any evidence of cannibalism. On the contrary, Walker (1983) notes that the Dorian Greek tradition of "*Omophagia*" was originally a cannibal orgy, in which the victims were ripped apart, and eaten raw.

MISSIONARY ZEAL IN DAHOMEY

Fig 8: Dieppe merchants of Portugal. The Portuguese s primary missin, was to target their religious propaganda towards the priests/ess, diviners, elders, and the nation s rulers. Believing that if they were successful in their conversion of them, the common people would automatically follow. Keeping in the tradition of their predecessors, these Dieppe merchants, in 1762, brought the first Euro-images of the *Madonna and child*, as a gift to King TegbŒsu of Dahomey. Shortly thereafter, they built their first Christian church at El Mina. One of the roles of this facility was to Christianized the captured Africans, waiting in their dungeons, to be transported across the Atlantic to the America s and enslaved. The Portuguese were the first to label African sacerdotal images as *fetishes*, which simply means *idols*. The Portugese were notorious for destroying the temples, images, and books of native peoples, whose philosophy and practices did not agree with their corrupted Christian doctrines. In Quidah, the Portuguese, French, British, Hollanders, and Danes, solicited Africans to build their fortress where they could engage in what was first slaves for weapons, gun power, textile etc. It later evolved into something far more horrendous., with the backing and blessings of the Holy Roman Imperial Church.

LE BOKONO

Fig 9: A diviner (Bokono) mocked as *Koukou-Charlatan*, (stupid fraud), as they have been so labeled by the French in Togo. In colonial Africa, these priest posed the greatest theat to colonial interest and a direct and deliberate campaign was implemented to discredit them. Sand divination by sand drawing is an ancient system invented by the black, matriarchal Korites, and other African clans of the southern Sudan and northeast Saudi Arabia.

THE NUTCRACKER

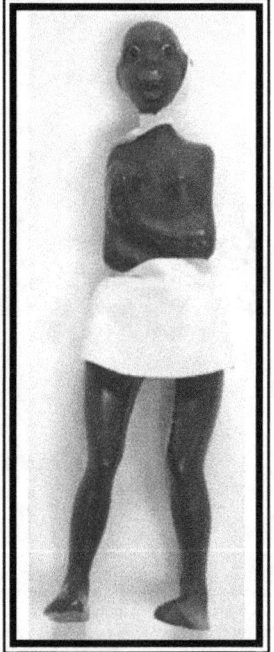

Fig 10: Nutcracker, made from wood or metal. Black woman dressed in ritual white. The nut is placed between her legs and squeezed to crack it.

THE CULTURAL REGULATORS

*"The prognathous [ape] race require
government also in their religious
exercises, or they degenerate to saturnalia*.
A discreet white man or woman should always
be present to regulate their religious meetings."*

E.N. Elliot, LL.D. Cotton is King 1860,

* *Saturnalia"*, was a major matriarchal, African and Tamil festive day celebrated, in ancient Greece to commemorate the safe journey of the Ancestors *Io/Onnaes/* from the flood.

Fig 11: BLACK WORSHIPERS REGULATED BY *WHITE OVERSEERS*

A typical scene experienced throughout the old South. Labeled as dark & dangerous, primitive, and demonic, Africans were never free to practice their spiritual traditions openly in America, earning them the dubious lable of being dark and maleficent.   A white overseer had to be present to make certain no African religious practices or liberation theology were being preached. This was so because when Africans prayed to *their own* angels [divinities], and Ancestors, they came to their aid. Such was the fear of whites, that even prayer by Africans was forbidden in many areas throughout the South. Gabriel, an *insurrectionist* known as the *Black Sampson*," is a case in point. Using familiar African coded, spiritual moral themes written in the Old Testament, Gabriel encouraged Africans to revolt.

Thousands eagerly complied in South Carolina, North Carolina, Georgia, Louisiana and Mississippi.[6] In that same time period, in 1831, in Southhampton, Virginia, an *"unmixed"*, enslaved African by the name of *Nat Turner*, possessed by the [Ancestral] "Spirits," staged an insurrection that left a trail of death and terror in its wake. Though unsuccessful, *Turner*'s actions terrorized every slaveholding state, leading them to strengthened their already oppressive Code Noir (Black Laws). Dehumanizing laws which declared in part that

"More than five male slaves were declared an unlawful assembly . . . neither slave nor free Negroes were permitted to preach unless before five respectable slave-holders and the Negroes so preaching were to be licensed by some neighboring religious society".[7]

Licensed by some neighboring religious society, meant that many Africa-Americans received their primary religious education from Black preachers who were coerced into sanctioning their forced bondage. A trend which continues unabated, even until today. The continued acceptance of Eurocentric, patriarchal theologies, has become a major dilemma for many African-Americans, who are actually descendants of Africans who were spiritually cultivated in either a largely matriarchal African society, or in a culture where the feminine principal as Goddess/Great Mother was highly venerated and respected.

THE "VOODOO" CURSE"
A film produced by Gordon Films-Galaworld Productions in 1965.

Fig 12: Cruse of the Voodoo"

Hollywood brain-washed generations all across the world to believe that African gnosis, ritual and spirituality were synonymous with evil, backwardness, supersitition and debauchery. Exemplified by the film synopsis which reads:

"*Bryant Holiday (Devil doll) and Dennis Price . . . While on a safari deep in the African jungle, a big-game hunter Mike Stacey, kills a sacred lion in the territory of the feared Simbazi tribe. The tribe places a voodoo curse on the hunter, vowing to torture and kill him by witchcraft. . . Can the great white hunter stop the jungle curse of the crazed Simbazi or will he be the next of an unspeakable voodooo vengeance?"*

The above film is typical of the racist and bigoted perceptions of African Spiritual gnosis as viewed by the Europeans and Christians, and promoted around the world as historical fact. If this same story were to be examined and interpreted from its African cosmological, religious and cultural perspective, it would reveal: A European foreigner, who intrudes upon the sacred African landscape, uninvited. His sole purpose is to maliciously murder a lion, an animal deemed a sacred symbol by the Simbazi clan, to take home as a prized-trophy. Because the European through his own racist attitudes, spiritual ignorance and careless actions demonstrates a lack of knowledge and respect for that which is sacred, he murders the lion, thus, causing the spirit of the Simbazi ancestors and the lion to lay claim to his soul for either restitution or retribution. A divine price he *must* pay in order to bring peace to the soul of the lion and to cool the wrath of the Simbazi ancestors. Instead, the European in his infinite arrogance, irrational fear and racial hatred, flees from his moral responsibility, and labels its spiritual aftermath as "evil", and the offended Africans as "crazed." A hauntingly symbolic and familiar theme that would repeat itself all throughout Africa's long and tumultuous history, with Europe and Europeans.

VOODOO MAMA/HOOCHIE MAMA /ANUNT JEMIMA/ HAG

Fig 13: "VOODOO 'ORGIASTIC' PRIESTESS"

Today's Americans are unaware that the sacred fertility dances performed by African women during ritual possession by their Divine African Mothers, and deities, and the European's ignorance and fear of them earned her, and the African Goddess, the reputation as the "*harlot, whore, prostitute*" etc.,. This attitude sanctioned the widespread rape, and perverted violation of black women's bodies during slavery, and Jim Crow. To prevent these violations, many generations of black women conditioned by these racists images, moved further away from their African roots, to mimic a "white irrational ideal" of sexual morality and femininity. Even until the present, black women's bodies are viewed as pornographic, and their gift to creatively swing, and gyrate their hips is viewed as "offensive."

VOODOO "*ORGIASTIC PRIESTESS*" THE TEMPLE "PROSTITUTE"

Fig 14: MOVIE POSTER WHICH READS *"SEX TO SEXY VOO DOO"* 99, TEMPLE PROSTITUTE

Above, the so-called "*temple prostitute*" so often thrown in the face of Africans by European writers who in their arrogance and ignorance, interpret African spiritual/ritual through their own sexually repressive and perverted lens. The role of the "*vestal virgin priestess*" has remained one of the most misunderstood aspects centering around the worship of the Divine African Mother. In truth, "*sacred prostitution*" had less to do with "*lust*" and "*immorality*," and everything to do with the sacred fertility rites, instituted to spread the ache (divine blood of the African Mother) through the general population. During African matriarchy, it was the mother's blood descent that was the most important. Many sacred kings and "saviors" were conceived in this fashion, to prevent sorcerers from learning the ethnic/clan identity of the father, lest they destroy their seed. It is believed that Christ was also conceived in this manner, thus, him never knowing his biological father, and being assigned one by religious revisionists. The Church later concealed this mode of conception by inventing the myth of "*Immaculate Conception*," and by replacing the ancient order of African vestal virgins into today's white, celibate nuns.

THE NUMBERS "WITCH"

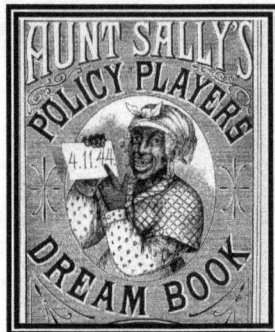

Fig 15: Old Hag

The use of numbers as a system of divination and magic have been in existence in Africa for centuries. The application of the magical and mystical value applied to numbers is as old as Africa herself. Born in the mystery schools and mother temples of ancient Egypt, Myceana, Ionia, and Asia Minor, the Egyptians, Sibyls and Chaldeans knew long before Pythagorus and Agrrippa, that the world was built upon the power of numbers. Africans enslaved in the New World were well familiar with the mystical power and use of numbers in working ritual as magic. Few Americans are even aware that it was African-Americans who invented the phenomenally successful gambling game of "*running numbers*," from which the lotto, and other games of chance are based. Black women prophetess, seers, and priestesses have been also divining with numbers for centuries. The deliberate depiction of the wise woman above as an "old witch/hag", is typical of how American culture strived to not only suppress and demonize black, feminine spiritual power and ritual mastery, but also to minimize its major contribution to Western popular metaphysical and occult sciences.

"THE SLAVE ASSEMBLE IN THE SWAMPS"

Peter Randolph, who grew up in slavery on a plantation in Prince George County, Virginia, received his freedom in 1847, following his owner's death, and then served as an anti-slavery agent, a newspaper editor, and as a Baptist minister in the North and in Canada. Following the Civil War, he served as minister in the Roland or Old African Baptist Church in Richmond, Virginia. This selection describes the disparity between the version of Christianity that masters taught to the slaves and the version that slaves taught to themselves:

Many say the Negroes receive religious education- - that Sabbath worship is instituted for them as for others, and were it not for slavery, they would die in their sins- - that really, the institution of slavery is a benevolent missionary enterprise. Yes, they are preached to, and I will give my readers some faint glimpses of these preachers, and their doctrines and practices.

Not being allowed to hold meetings on the plantation, the slaves assemble in the swamps, out of reach of the patrols. They have an understanding among themselves as to the time and place of getting together. This is often done by the first one arriving breaking boughs from the trees, and bending them in the direction of the selected spot. Arrangements are then made for conducting the exercises. They first ask each other how they feel, the state of their minds, etc. The male members then select a certain space, in separate groups, for their division of the meeting. Preaching in order, by the brethren; then praying and singing all round, until they generally feel quite happy. The speaker usually commences by calling himself unworthy, and talks very slowly, until, feeling the spirit, he grows excited, and in a short time, there fall to the ground twenty or thirty men and women under its influence. Enlightened people call it excitement . . . The slave forgets all his sufferings, except to remind others of the trials during the past week, exclaiming: 'Thank God, I shall not live here always!' Then they pass from one to another, shaking hands, and bidding each other farewell, promising, should they meet no more on earth, to strive and meet in heaven, where all is joy, happiness and liberty. As they separate, they sing a parting hymn of praise. Sometimes the slaves meet in an old log- cabin, when they find it necessary to keep a watch. If discovered, they escape, if possible; but those who are caught often get whipped. . . Most of the songs used in worship are composed by the slaves themselves, and describe their own sufferings.

In some places, if the slaves are caught praying to God, they are whipped more than if they had committed a great crime. The slave-holders will allow the slaves to dance, but do not want them to pray to God. Sometimes, when a slave, on being whipped, calls upon God, he is forbidden to do so, under threat of having his throat cut, or brains blown out. Oh, reader! this seems very hard- - that slaves cannot call on their Maker, when the case most needs it. Sometimes the poor slave takes courage to ask his master to let him pray, and is driven away, with the answer, that if discovered praying, his back will pay the bill.

Peter Randolph, 1825?-1897
"Slave Cabin to the Pulpit."
The Autobiography of Rev. Peter Randolph

The Mockery of Religious Freedom in America

Headlines read: *"Special to the New York Times"*, dated Friday, August 14, 1925. Caption reads: *"Seize Price Lists of Voodoo Doctor: Police get Circulars Offering "Wishing Dust, and Lucky Charms to Negroes at $1 to $10000.*

> THE NEW YORK TIMES, FRIDAY, AUGUST 14, 1925
>
> **SEIZE PRICE LISTS OF VOODOO DOCTOR**
>
> *Police Get Circulars Offering 'Wishing Dust' and Lucky Charms to Negroes at $1 to $1,000.*
>
> Special to The New York Times.
> ATLANTIC CITY, Aug. 13.—Twelve thousand circulars said to have been sent to this city by a New York voodoo doctor were seized by the police here today as they were being distributed to negro homes on the north side by six negro boys.
> The circulars bore the address of D. Alexander of 99 Downing Street, Brooklyn, N. Y.
> All sorts of love powders, wishing dust, lucky charms and incantations are offered for sale on the circular, with prices ranging from $1 to $1,000.
> "Guffer Dust, New Moon, No. 1 good, $60; Happy Dust, $40; Black Cats Ankle Dust, $500; Black Cat's Wishbone, $1,000; King Solomon's Marrow, $1,000; Easy Life Powder, $100; Tying Down Goods, $50; Chasing Away Goods, $50; Hoss Fix Powders, $15, and Buzzard Nest, $100," were some of the goods offered.
> Inquiry developed that "Bringing Back Powders" were designed to return an errant wife or husband to a grieving spouse, "Tying Down Goods" were said to keep the object of one's affections from departing, while "Chasing Away Goods" had the opposite effect. "Boss Fix Powders" keep one's employer in a friendly mood.
> At 99 Downing Street, Brooklyn, a three-story frame building, the name "D. Alexander" was on the windows of a locked store in the basement. Bottles of fluids and powders were displayed there. Persons in the house above professed ignorance of the basement's occupant.

Fig 16: Religious persecution

By the early 1900s, the religion of Vodoun had been successfully maligned and forced underground, and its outward practices eliminated or forgotten entirely by the younger African American generations. It was also during this time that African-Americans were experiencing unprecedented theft and illegal seizures of their land in the South. The Folk-Medicine and ethno-botanical magic that remained, known to most as "Hoodoo and Conjuration," is a rich, cultural folk-magical, tradition practiced all over the African continent since time immemorial. In the U.S., this practice was mislabeled and universally regarded as the so-called "Voodoo" religion.

Because African-Americans were denied quality heath care, and legal representation, the Folk-doctors and Conjurers became essential. These traditions rooted in African theology, philosophy, culture, ancestral power and magical ethno-botanical knowledge were fused with Native American ethnobotany, and concealed under acceptable European folklore which ironically, is derived from ancient African old world beliefs. Because African-Americans were routinely denied proprietary licenses to open businesses in their own communities, the supplies needed to practice this folk art were sold in botanicas, mainly monopolized by Jewish merchants.

Just as with Vodoun and its priesthoods, African-American "Hoodoo" priests and priestesses were routinely harassed, and put out of business, or exposed as "quacks and frauds." African-Americans were forced to "sneak and hide" or made to feel "immoral, unrighteous, non-Christian," if "caught visiting these priests, or seen purchasing or empowering themselves with their wares. Ironically, today, "hoodoo" passing as "Voodoo" and lacking the sacred power and knowledge of its forebears is the fastest growing magical tradition practiced by non-African-Americans.

WHO INVENTED THE KOLA BEVERAGE?

ENSLAVED "ROOTWOMAN" INVENTOR OF COCA-COLA?

Fig17. Caption: *"The Native are restless for Afri-Cola. Five Jungle flavors. It Sothes the Savage thirst!*

Perhaps the entire world is indebted to the enslaved Africans in America from among other things, the probable invention of the world's most favorite and addictive beverage, "Coca Cola." Its main ingredient the "Kola Nut," is native to West Africa, and has been in use not only in West Africa, but by all of Africa since time immemorial. Known as *"bisi or goro"* to the Ewe, and "bese" in Ghana, "guiti" in Benin, oji" to the Hausa and Igbo, and "boroji, obi, goro" in N. Nigeria, this bitter 2-4 lobbed fruit was imported and used extensively by Africans enslaved in America. From the *Sterculiaceae* family, it is grown from a variety of evergreen species, (Cola nitida), cultivated and sold in the West African markets by the Hausa and Yoruba. (Ayensu, 1978, p. 255; Mshana, N.R., et. al., 2000, p. 565).

(cont)

(Cont)   TRADITIONAL USES

The Kola Nut is especially sacred in both the Vodoun tradition of West Africa and of the Diaspora, the Ifa'Orisha of the Yoruba, the spiritual traditions of the Igbo in southeastern Nigeria, Ghana, Ivory Coast etc.,. One of its main active ingredients being caffeine. As a medicine, the seeds are used as a tonic, stimulant, diuretic, anti-depressant, and to treat dysentery, herpes, fractures, nausea, indigestion, fatigue, hunger, labor pains and even as a aphrodisiac. (Ibid.) Its roots are used as a dentifrice (chewing sticks) and mouth sanitizer. Its bark is used to make ceremonial objects, boats and furniture. For religious purposes, it is offered as a holy sacrament, and as food to the ancestors, divinities and as a tool for divination. Culturally, it is used in West Africa as part of a dowry proceeding marriage, or given as a wedding gift, and is often used as a peace maker in settling disputes. It is the main ingredient in the world's most widely drank and popular beverage, Cola-Cola.

Fig 18

MYTHS OF COCA-COLA'S AMERICAN ORIGINS

There are two versions of how Cola-Cola was invented. The "official verison" claims that when the enslaved Africans brought the four-seeded pods to America, its medicinal and healing properties were suddenly recognized and discovered by a local, white Georgia pharmacist named, *John Pemberton*, who, through "trail and error", discovered that by mixing the ground seed with sugar and soda water, it produced a nerve stimulate and tonic. Thus, Coca-Cola was born. However, in the "Black verison," it is believed that a rootwoman, enslaved as a house servant, would make the tonic, to relieve the depression and indigestion of her "master." In doing this, it would prevent his usual violent outbursts, and the slaves would be spared his brutality. So impressed was he with the healing beverage, that he took it to the local pharmacists to determine its ingredients and how to
mass produce it. Thus, Coca-Cola was born.

Fig 18: "Toni-Kola". Vintage poster of popular West African and French cola

Re-Education
THE TRUTH ABOUT YEVEH MAMI WATA VODOUN

Fig 19: Mama Zogbé (Mamaissii Vivian Hunter-Hindrew) giving presentation on Mami Wata and Yeveh Vodoun religion. © Mama Zogbé (Mamaissii Vivian Hunter-Hindrew)

"*It is important to re-educate the Diaspora and the general public the truth about Vodoun and Mami Wata. It is time for African Religions to be accorded the same respect, and exposure that other religions have enjoyed for so long. The Vodoun and other African based traditions are the birth-right and the true divine power of the Diaspora. The more they learn they more they will understand and realize what they and their children have been missing.*" -Mama Zogbé (Mamaissii Vivian Hunter-Hindrew)

Fig 20: © Mama Zogbé (Vivian Hunter-Hindrew), Atlanta conference © MWHS

35 RACISM & RELIGIOUS PERSECUTION

NOTES:

1. Matthews, Terry. Professor. *The Religion of the Slaves.* (see online resources bibliography).
2. Ibid.
3. Keltie, J. Scott. *Africa.* Keller, G. Albert ed. *History of Nations* Vol XIX. New York: P.F. Collier & Sons Company, 1928. p. 15, 140 185.
4. Matthews.
5. Ibid.
6. Slavery and Religion in America: A Time Line 1440-1866. Internet Public Library. (see online resources bibliography).
7. Cromwell, W. John. *"The Aftermath of Nat Turner's Insurrection."* The Journal of Negro History. V.1 (1920): 208-234.

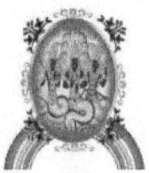

CHIEF HOUNON- AMENGANSIE PRIESTESS

Mama Zogbé

Mama Zogbé (legal name, Vivian Hunter-Hindrew) is a fully initiated *Hounon-Amengansie* (High Priestess) of the Amengansie, Ancestral Tchamba, West African Vodoun, Mami Wata, and Afa (Ifa) healing traditions. She resides in the United States, where she maintains her ancestral shines and works full-time as an Amengansie Vodoun priestess and godmother.

Mama Zogbé, African-American

Born from the womb of Mami Wata and the Vodoun, Mama Zogbé's spiritual lineage descends directly from both sides of her maternal and paternal great grandmothers and fathers, who were Mami Wata & Vodoun priests, captured & enslaved as hired-out masons and carvers in Louisiana. During Slavery and Reconstruction, African descendants were forbidden to practice their ancestral religions, many were persecuted and murdered. Such was the case in the family of Mama Zogbé where her great-grandfather, *Prince Hunter*, was killed in Natchitoches, Parish in Louisiana. Family lore recounts that he refusing to convert to Christianity, was chased into a barn and set-ablaze.

Over time, the Vodoun tradition was forced underground and a deliberate process of mockery and racist malignment began in American media, religious and educational institutions, creating some of the most perverse, undeserved and enduring stereotypes of African religions, which has continued unabated until the present.

After more than 30 years of intense manifestational encounters, and personal suffering, Mama Zogbé received her first ceremonies in Togo West Africa, by Hounon Togbui (Master), Akuete Durchbach (1988), and full initiations by Hounons Togbuis Arita & Daniel Sossah In Togo, and the U.S. (1996). She completed her final series of ceremonies as Chief Hounon Amengansie in 2003-2005.

As a full-lineage African-American priestess, Mama Zogbé is the first to initiate many in the Diaspora to Mami Wata, Mama Tchamba, Vodoun and Amengansie tradition. She is a graduate of Chaminade University (Honolulu, HI, 1981, BGS), and Augusta State University (GA: 1995 M.Ed.). She is world traveled (South America, France, Italy, Czechoslovakia, Germany, Austria, Mexico, Ghana, Cote d'Ivoire, and others). She has been traveling to Togo, West Africa regularly since 1988.

Mama Zogbe is also the founder and president of the first non-profit, 501(c)3, **Mami Wata Healing Society of North America, Inc.**, (formerly **OATH:** *Organization of African Traditional Healers*), which recently won a long overdue victory with the U.S. Library of Congress, in changing the classification of African Traditional Religions, from the historically derisive label of *Occult/Satanism* to *African Spirituality, Religion, and African-American Studies*. *Her hopes that her two-volume well researched book: Mami Wata: An Ancient African God/dess Unveiled" can be used as an instrument to shed much needed history and accurate knowledge on African ancient traditional religions and their crucial but long omitted role in laying the theological, ritual and cultural foundation of the major religions throughout the ancient world.*

TO REQUEST SPEAKING ENGAGEMENTS PLEASE VISIT

www.mamiwata.com/speaker.html

P.O. Box 211281 * Martinez, GA 30907
Chief Hounon-Amengansie, Mama Zogbé. Main Shrine: (706) 267-3324   Apokassii, Hounon-Amengansie: (678) 358-0620
Fax: (706) 267-3324* Website: www.mamiwata.com

MAMA ZOGBÉ
CHIEF HOUNON-AMENGANSIE, OF MAMI WATA YEVEH VODOUN

FOR APPOINTMENT:
(706) 267-3324

EMAIL:
INFO@MAMIWATA.COM

OFFERING POWERFUL, PROFESSIONAL & CONFIDENTIAL SPIRITUAL SERVICES YEAR ROUND

By Appointment Only!

♦ **DIVINATIONS:** (SPIRITUAL READINGS)

CALLING-ÜP THE DEAD AND THE LIVING . . .

- ♦ CALL-UP DECEASED FAMILY MEMBERS FOR CONSULTATIONS
- ♦ CALL-UP ORI (PERSONAL SOUL/SPIRIT) FOR CONSULTATIONS
- ♦ CALL-UP ALL VODOU, ORISHAS, NKISI, ABOSOMS ETC., FOR CONSULTATION
- ♦ CALL-UP ORI (PERSONAL SOUL) OF LOST/ MISSING FAMILY MEMBERS
- ♦ CALL-UP MURDERED FAMILY MEMBERS FOR CONSULTATIONS
- ♦ CALL-UP FAMILY MEMBERS IN COMA FOR CONSULTATIONS

POWERFÜL RITÜAL . . .

CLEANSINGS/HEALINGS:

- ♦ POWERFUL RITUAL HEALING /EXORCISM CLEANSING BATHS
- ♦ MAMI WATA RITUAL OFFERINGS
- ♦ ANCESTRAL TCHAMBA HEALINGS (All Addictions, Family fighting, etc.,)

INITIATIONS:

- ♦ INSTALL ALL VODOU, MAMA TCHAMBA (divine slave ancestors)
- ♦ ALL DAN'S (RAINBOW SERPENT DEITIES)
- ♦ MAMI WATA , AMENGANSIE
  - ♦ AHOLU/SAKPATA (MOTHER/FATHER EARTH DEITY OF DISEASE & HEALING)
  - ♦ TCHAMBA (ANCESTRAL SHRINES)

Serious Inquiries ONLY!
MAMI WATA HEALERS SOCIETY OF NORTH AMERICA INC.,
P.O. Box 211281
MARTINEZ, GA 30907
HQTS: (706) 267-3324
Fax: (706) 863-4886
MWHS@MAMIWATA.COM

WEBSITE: WWW.MAMIWATA.COM

FOR APPOINTMENT: (706) 267-3324
EMAIL: INFO@MAMIWATA.COM

Mami Wata Healers Society of North America

Presents

Other educational books by Mama Zogbé

Volume I
ISBN: 978-0-9716-2457-30
ISBN: 0 0-9716245-7-7
565 pages, 6" x 9"
Price: $53.33

Volume II
ISBN: 978-0-9716-2458-
368 pages, 6" x 9"
Price: $30.64

Available online:

http://www.lulu.com/content/982462
http://www.lulu.com/content/983287
Amazon.com

Please contact your local bookstores as request that they stock these books!

Support African Religions. Visit our online store!

http://www.cafepress.com/mamiwata

www.ingramcontent.com/pod-product-compliance
Lightning Source LLC
Chambersburg PA
CBHW031207160426
43193CB00008B/539